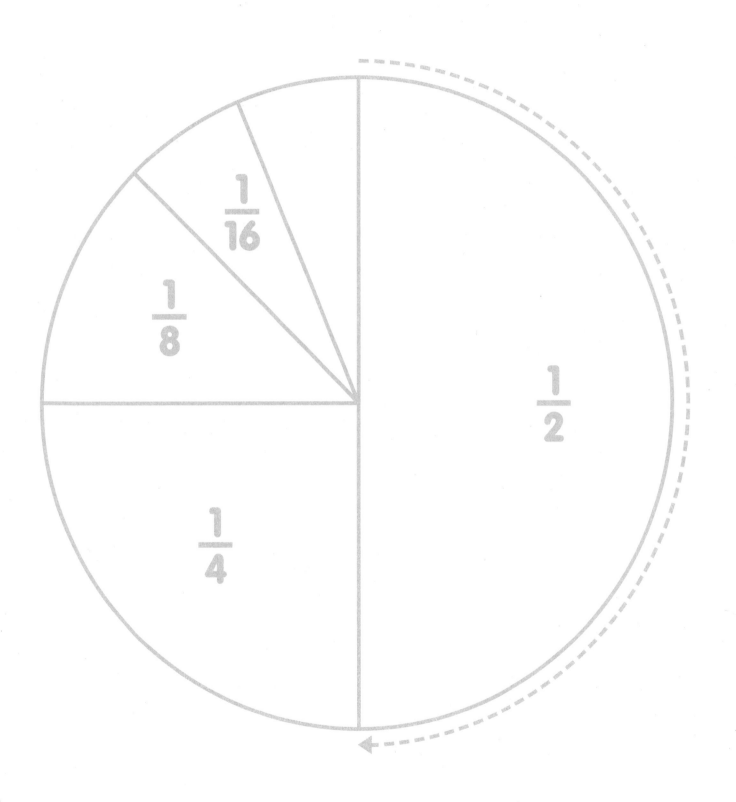

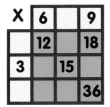

Carol Vorderman's

Maths Made Easy

London • New York • Sydney • Delhi

A DORLING KINDERSLEY BOOK
www.dk.com

Text: Sean McArdle

Senior Editor: Sue Leonard
Senior Art Editor: Marcus James
Designers: Cathy Chesson,
Carole Oliver, Jane Tetzlaff
Digital Artworks: Robin Hunter
DTP Designer: Almudena Díaz
Production: Josie Alabaster
Managing Editor: Mary Ling
Managing Art Editor: Rachael Foster

First published in Great Britain in 1999
by Dorling Kindersley Limited
9 Henrietta Street, London WC2E 8PS

2 4 6 8 10 9 7 5 3 1

Copyright © 1999
Dorling Kindersley Limited, London

A CIP catalogue record for this book is
available from the British Library.

ISBN 0 7513 5667 0

Colour reproduction by Mullis Morgan, London
Printed and bound in Italy by L.E.G.O.

Contents

Introduction

This book is going to make maths easy for you. In our daily lives we use words all the time and often take them for granted. But when it comes to numbers a lot of people claim they can't work them out. But just like words, numbers are all around us and we need to understand how to use them to do all sorts of everyday things – from measuring to multiplying and map-reading – and for some, there are exams to pass, too! The vital thing to remember is that numbers are not mysterious things and that by learning about them in a simple, straightforward, fresh new way you can come to grips with them and make them work for you. Look at and learn about all of the basic maths concepts explained here and discover that maths really couldn't be easier. You *can* do it!

Carol Vorderman

Addition 1

There are many words that mean "add" or "adding". All of the following words can be used: plus, more, sum, total, together, altogether, increase.

Adding in disguise

Adding sums can be written in different ways. If you need to add the number of red paint brushes to the number of blue ones, you could write the sum like this:

3 more than **7**   The total of **3** and **7**

Increase **3** by **7**   The sum of **3** and **7**

Adding across and down

Sums can be written in two ways.

3 + 7 = 10

This is called horizontal addition.

$$+\ \frac{3}{10}\ 7$$

This is called vertical addition.

Adding larger numbers

You need to use vertical addition when you are adding larger numbers. When you write the sum vertically, put the numbers under columns for hundreds, tens, and units, like this:

Add up the 2,1, and 1 to make 400.

The units add up to 10, so you need to carry over the 1 to the tens column. Put the 1 under the line and add it to the 5 and 4. It makes 10 again. So carry over the 1 into the hundreds column.

Adding up thousands

Add thousands up in the same way as you do for hundreds, tens, and units. Just add an extra column beside the hundreds. Remember to carry the one wherever you have to and add it to the other numbers in the next column.

The units add up to 15, so you need to carry over the 1 into the tens column.

Put the 1 under the line and add it to the 5 and 1.

Now try these
326 + 218   457 + 336
3174 + 1926

Number bonds

If you know the answer to some simple additions off by heart, it will help with harder problems later on. Common pairs of numbers that are added together are called number bonds. You should know all the number bonds with answers up to 20. Practise if you don't.

Now try these

$7 + 8$ $6 + 9$ $5 + 8$ $4 + 3$

$6 + 7$ $2 + 8$ $9 + 5$ $7 + 1$

Using number bonds

Number bonds can help you to add horizontally. Let's try 37 + 8.

First think of **37** as **30** and **7**.

Now use number bonds to work out that **7** and **8** are **15**.

Finally, add the **15** and the **30**. The answer is **45**.

Carol's tips

" If you are adding up a list of numbers, write them in a column. Add them up in the normal way from top to bottom. To check the answer, add from the bottom upwards. The two answers should be the same. "

Now try these

$18 + 9$ $38 + 7$ $24 + 8$ $54 + 9$

Adding a 9, or numbers that end in 9

If you want to add a **9** to a number, you can begin by adding **10** and then taking away **1**.

Work out **26 + 9** by adding **26 + 10** to make **36**. Then take away **1** which is **35**.

Now try these

$38 + 19$ $65 + 29$ $46 + 39$ $38 + 59$

Common pairs of numbers that are added together are called number bonds.

$3 + 2 = 5$

Addition 2

Learning to add combinations of numbers in different ways helps you tackle sums that may seem difficult at first. It will also help you with mental maths.

   **+**

Another way to add

Big numbers look more difficult to add up than single units, but there are ways of simplifying the sums. Let's try adding 668 and 866.

> **668 + 866**

First add the hundreds	600 + 800 = 1400
Next add the tens	60 + 60 = 120
Then add the units	8 + 6 = 14
Finally, add them all up	1534

> **Carol's tips**
> "You may see thousands written with a space: 1 456, or sometimes with a comma: 1,456. Tens of thousands are usually written with a space: 10 000. "

Now try these   437 + 265   743 + 185   518 + 367

Estimating answers

> **218 + 390**

For adding sums, it is useful to see what the answer is *likely to be*. This is called estimating. *An estimate is a clever guess.* You can do it by "rounding" numbers up or down to the nearest ten or hundred.

Try adding 218 and 390.

218 is about **200**
390 is about **400**

So the answer will be about **600**

If the answer you work out is a long way off your estimate, you will know you have made a mistake. (The answer is 608.)

Now try these

613 + 192

304 + 509

108 + 394

216 + 494

The idea of going to the nearest ten or hundred is called "rounding".

Adding mentally

Knowing number bonds, rounding numbers, and estimating answers are all methods that will help you to add. There are two more methods. Let's try with 45 + 38.

> **45 + 38**

First add the **8** to **45**	**8 + 45 = 53**
Now add the **30** to the **53**	**30 + 53 = 83**

This is the two-stage method.

Let's try it another way:

First add **40** and **30**	**40 + 30 = 70**
Now add **5** and **8**	**5 + 8 = 13**
Finally, add **70** and **13**	**70 + 13 = 83**

This is the three-stage method.

Carol's tips

"When you have lists of numbers to add up, look for numbers that add up to 10, even though they may not be next to one another. For example, add 3, 9, and 7. The 3 and 7 make 10. Then it's easy to add on the 9 to make 19."

Now try these

27 + 45   54 + 39

36 + 57   63 + 23

Columns

Be careful when you are adding numbers of different sizes such as 246 + 78. When this happens you must make sure you write the numbers in the correct places in the correct columns.

> **246 + 78**

$$\begin{array}{r} 246 \\ +78 \\ \hline 324 \end{array}$$

$$\begin{array}{r} 246 \\ +78 \\ \hline 1026 \end{array} \text{WRONG}$$

Now try these

26 + 437   2453 + 316

Adding decimals

Adding decimals is as easy as ordinary adding, as long as you *keep the decimals in the correct columns*. If you want to know how far the boy on the left is reaching, write out the sum: 1.44 + .60.

> **1.44 + .60**

$$\begin{array}{r} 1.44 \\ +.60 \\ \hline 2.04 \end{array}$$

$$\begin{array}{r} 1.44 \\ +.60 \\ \hline 744 \end{array} \text{WRONG}$$

Now try these

4.76 + 0.38   3.53 + 1.65

0.6 m

1.44 m

Always keep decimals in the correct columns when adding.

Subtraction

The word "subtract" will not always appear in a sum or problem so you'll need to know other words and phrases that mean the same thing. The following expressions can be used: minus, take away, how much less, difference between, reduce by, how many are left, decrease.

Subtracting by building

A very good method of subtracting mentally is called "building" or "counting up". Let's subtract 72 from 99.

Begin by counting up from **72**	**72 to 80 =**	8
Now count up from **80**	**80 to 90 =**	10
Then build up from **90**	**90 to 99 =**	9
Finally, add up the bits		27

Carry the 1 across.

Now try these 43 – 25   61 – 37   52 – 16   86 – 59

Taking away vertically

A golden rule to start with: always take bottom from top. Subtraction is easy when the bottom number is smaller than the top number. It's harder when it's the other way around. When the bottom number is larger, you need to exchange with the next column. Some people call this "borrowing" but really you are "exchanging". When you exchange, you convert a ten into ten units, or a hundred into ten tens.

The number you exchange with will go down by 1, so the 5 becomes 4.

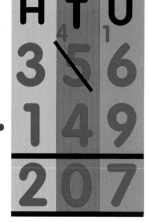

The number you give to will go up by 10, so the 6 becomes 16.

Now try these 428 – 319   371 – 154   517 – 348

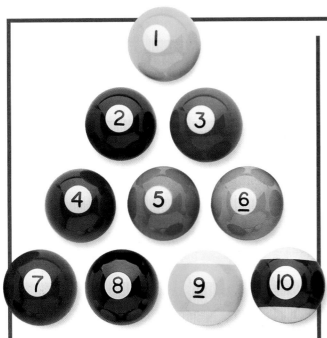

Subtracting 9

If you need to subtract 9, just take away 10 and then add 1 back on. 56 – 9 could be worked out as:

$$56 - 10 = 46$$
$$46 + 1 = 47$$

Subtracting 11

> 73 – 11

If you need to subtract 11, just take away 10 and then take away another 1. 73 – 11 could be worked out as:

$$73 - 10 = 63$$
$$63 - 1 = 62$$

Now try these
$$33 - 9 \quad 42 - 11$$
$$42 - 9 \quad 67 - 11$$
$$64 - 9 \quad 33 - 11$$

Awkward subtractions

> 306 – 148

Probably the most awkward subtractions are when there's a zero on the top line. Let's subtract 148 from 306.

You need to exchange with the zero, which is impossible, so you need a new plan.

You first have to exchange with the 3 and give ten tens to the zero. Make sure you change the 3 to 2 because you exchanged with it.

Now you can exchange with the tens column because you have 10 there. The 6 becomes 16.

The 10 becomes 9.

Now the sum can be finished normally.

Now try these
$$307 - 149 \quad 602 - 435$$
$$470 - 248 \quad 320 - 106$$

Checking answers

The answer to the subtraction on the right is 118. To be sure of this, add 118 to the amount you took away. The total should be the figure in the top line.

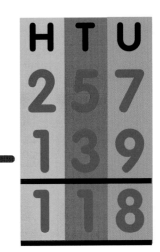

$$118 + 139 = 257$$

Multiplication 1

Adding is a way of making numbers grow slowly.
Multiplication is a way of making numbers grow more quickly.

Multiplying is convenient

> **7 × 4**

Let's look at these bug-laden leaves. If you want to find out how many bugs there are altogether, you could add 7 + 7 + 7 + 7. That takes time. It's quicker if you know that 7 x 4 = 28.

Multiplying by a single digit

> **273 × 6**

This method is fairly simple as long as you remember your times tables. For this sum you need to know your six times table.

Make sure you put the numbers in the correct columns.

	Th	H	T	U
		2	7	3
×				6

		Th	H	T	U
First multiply the **3** by **6**				1	8
Now multiply the **70** by **6**			4	2	0
Now multiply the **200** by **6**		1	2	0	0
Finally, add them all together		1	6	3	8

The 3 is in the units column, so you multiply 3 by 6.

The 7 is in the tens column, so you multiply 70 by 6.

The 2 is in the hundreds column, so you multiply 200 by 6.

Now try these 146 x 4 314 x 6 265 x 5 472 x 7

Multiplying by 10 or 100 or 1 000

When you multiply a whole number by ten, or a multiple of ten, just add the same number of zeros to that number. Like this:

7 × 10 = 70 — *Just add 0 to the 7.*

7 × 100 = 700 — *Just add 00 to the 7.*

7 × 1 000 = 7 000 — *Just add 000 to the 7.*

Carol's tips
" Multiplying by zero means having no lots of whatever the number is. So no lots of anything equals nothing! Try multiplying 7 x 0, 11 x 0, or 15 x 0. The answer should always be zero! "

Remember that multiplication is really repeated addition.

Multiplying with larger numbers

It is easier to understand this multiplying method if you think of 13 as 10 + 3.

> **246 × 13**

	Th	H	T	U
		2	4	6
×			1	3

First multiply the **246** by **3**	7 3 8
Now multiply the **246** by **10**	2 4 6 0
Finally, add them together	3 1 9 8

Carry the 1 over. ⌐1

Now try these **157 × 15** **123 × 14**

Multiplying by 20, 30, 40...

It's useful to know that when you multiply a number by ten, you just put a zero on the end of the number. You can use that idea again for 20, 30, 40, and beyond. For 23 × 20, think of 20 as 10 × 2.

> **23 × 20**

Think of 20 as 10 × 2.

First multiply the **23** by **10**	230
Then, multiply **230** by **2**	460

Now try these **13 × 20** **14 × 20** **12 × 40** **13 × 50**

Doubling up!

Doubling numbers is a very useful skill and quite easy to do in your head. To work out 34 × 2, begin by thinking of 34 as 30 + 4.

> **34 × 2**

Think of 34 as 30 + 4.

First double the **30**	60
Next double the **4**	8
Finally, add them together	68

Multiplying by 4

To multiply any large number by 4, first double each figure and then double it again. Let's try multiplying 142 × 4.

> **142 × 4**

Each figure represents hundreds, tens, or units.

First double **100** = **200** and double again	400
Next double **40** = **80** and double again	160
Then double **2** = **4** and double again	8
Finally, add them all together	568

Now try these **18 × 4** **247 × 4** **362 × 4** **163 × 4**

The product is the answer you get when you multiply two or more numbers.

Multiplication 2

Multiplying with decimals is like normal multiplication, except you need to remember where to put the decimal point. It's important to check your answers by estimating.

Multiplying with decimals

You use decimals when you are doing calculations with money, so getting the answer right is very important. To work out how much you will spend on four kites if a kite costs £9.87, do the calculation vertically. When you have found the answer, check how many figures were behind the decimal point to start with. There were two. This means there must be two numbers behind the point in the answer.

> **£9.87 x 4**

$$
\begin{array}{r}
9.87 \\
\times \quad 4 \\
\hline
39.48 \\
\hline
\end{array}
$$

There are two figures behind the decimal point…

…so there should be two figures behind the decimal point in the answer.

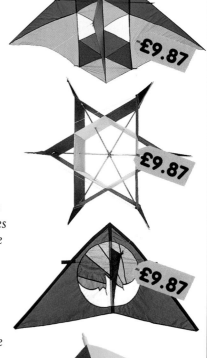

£9.87

£9.87

£9.87

£9.87

Carol's tips
66 When multiplying 10 by another 10, or by 100, or a 1 000, you can check your answer by making sure you have the same number of zeros in the answer as in the whole of the sum. 99

Make sure you're correct

Estimating is helpful when multiplying decimals. Estimate how much the four kites would cost like this:

£9.87 is close to **£10**, so **£10 x 4** is **£40**.

So your answer should be about **£40**. In fact, the answer is **£39.48**. Make sure the point is in the right place, otherwise your answer could be as high as **£3 948**! The same principle applies even when you are not calculating with money.

Now try these **3.9 x 7 4.7 x 4 5.5 x 5 8.4 x 8**

Remember to check the position of the decimal point.

To multiply by 10 the numbers have to move one place to the left.

Multiplying by 10

When you multiply decimals by 10, the numbers move one place to the left. In the same way, when you multiply by 100 the numbers move two places to the left.

Now try these 4.8×10 5.84×10 72.3×100

Length and weight

As well as money, decimals are often used with measurements of length and weight. As long as you follow the simple ideas on the left you should be all right. Remember to estimate first.

9.25 cm has two numbers to the right of the point, so the answer is 27.75 cm

$$\begin{array}{r} 9.25 \text{ cm} \\ \times\ 3 \\ \hline 15 \\ 60 \\ 2700 \\ \hline 27.75 \end{array}$$

$$\begin{array}{r} 1.7 \text{ kg} \\ \times 8 \\ \hline 56 \\ 80 \\ \hline 13.6 \end{array}$$

1.7 kg has one number to the right of the point, so the answer is 13.6 kg

Carol's tips

"When you multiply decimal amounts it can be useful to change the units. For example, 1.6 cm x 0.4 cm might look worrying, so you could change them both to millimetres (16 x 4). But remember to change the answer back to centimetres."

You might need to multiply decimals when you're measuring length.

A multiplying game

This is a fun way of multiplying, which is useful for checking answers. To work out 136 x 4, multiply 1, 3, and 6 by 4 and put the numbers of the answer on either side of a diagonal line.

$$136 \times 4$$

$1 \times 4 = 04$, so insert 0 and 4. $3 \times 4 = 12$, so insert 1 and 2. $6 \times 4 = 24$, so insert 2 and 4.

Add up the numbers in the triangles to find the answer, which is 544.

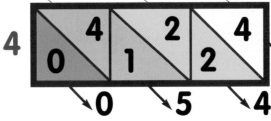

Division 1

All of the following words are connected with division: share, group, divide, factor, into, lots of. It's important to make sure you can recognize each one so that you know when you should be dividing.

12

− 3

To work out 12 divided by 3, you can keep taking away 3 until you reach zero.

Division or subtraction?

You can think of dividing as subtracting until you reach zero.
If you have 12 model soccer players and want to know how many groups of three they make, you can find out by subtracting three until you reach zero.

12 ÷ 3

− 3

This shows that 4 lots of 3 are the same as 12, so 12 divided by 3 is 4.

− 3 = 0

Division and fractions

Division and fractions are connected. If you need to find ½ of something, it means you need to divide the number or amount by 2. If it's ¼, you have to divide by 4.

1 $\frac{1}{2}$ $\frac{1}{4}$

Now try these   What is $\frac{1}{2}$ of **60?**   What is $\frac{1}{3}$ of **24?**   What is $\frac{1}{4}$ of **80?**

Which sign?

Both of these signs: ÷ and ⌐ mean divide.

20 ÷ 4

This means divide 20 by 4.

4⌐20

This means "how many 4s in 20?"

Carol's tips

❝If you know your times tables, you will know the answers to lots of division sums! If you know that 6 x 3 is 18, you also know that 18 ÷ 3 is 6 and 18 ÷ 6 is 3.❞

Now try these

7⌐28   56 ÷ 7   32 ÷ 4   6⌐36

Remember that dividing is simply repeated subtraction.

Remainders

It would be great if all division sums worked out exactly, but they don't. Sometimes there are bits left over and we call these bits remainders. To make life easier we write "r" instead of "remainder". Take a look at how many buttons are left over when 11 buttons are divided into groups of three.

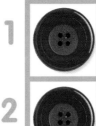

Remainder 2

$$11 \div 3 = 3 \; r \; 2$$

Short division

Short division means dividing by just one number. Sometimes this can be done in your head, but the work often needs to be written down. This is the usual way to do short division.

$7 \overline{)238}$

How many 7s in 2? There are none.

How many 7s in 23? There are 3, with 2 remaining.

0 3 4

$7 \overline{)23\,^28}$

Put the remainder 2 next to the 8.

You have to divide the 7 into 2, 23, and 28.

How many 7s in 28? There are 4, so the answer is 34.

Carol's tips

" Dividing an even number by two will always work out exactly:

$$26 \div 2 = 13$$
$$94 \div 2 = 47.$$

Dividing an odd number by two will always give ½ in the answer:

$$49 \div 2 = 24½$$
$$17 \div 2 = 8½. \text{"}$$

Now try these $8 \overline{)594}$ $7 \overline{)364}$ $6 \overline{)468}$ $7 \overline{)616}$

Dividing mentally

This takes a bit of thought – take it slowly. You should be able to work out the sums on the right in your head.

Now try these

$3 \overline{)135}$ $5 \overline{)75}$ $7 \overline{)84}$

$4 \overline{)96}$ $6 \overline{)144}$ $8 \overline{)128}$

Knowing your times tables will help you with division.

$45 \div 3 = 15$

Division 2

Division is something you use all the time, whether you're dividing a group of friends into teams or splitting the cost of a pizza. So make sure you get it right!

Sensible division

In real life, some division answers are a bit silly. Here's an example. A teacher can fit 12 pencils in one jar. How many jars will he need for 18 pencils? Well, 18 divided by 12 is 1½, but half a jar won't be very useful.

Of course, the teacher will really need two jars.

Now try these A minibus carries 10 children, but 15 need to travel. How many buses are needed? A vase can hold up to 15 roses. How many vases will be needed for 80 roses?

Dividing by 10

When a number is divided by 10 it becomes 10 times smaller. This means that $80 \div 10$ becomes 8. Remember that all whole numbers can be written with a decimal point at the end. So, 23 is the same as 23.0. It's useful to use decimal points when you're dividing by 10. The easiest way is to move the numbers one place to the right.

$$23 \div 10$$

$$23.0 \div 10 = 2.3$$

The numbers have moved one place to the right.

$$283.0 \div 10 = 28.3$$

The numbers have moved one place to the right.

Dividing by 100

When a number is divided by 100 it becomes 100 times smaller. This means that $600 \div 100$ becomes 6. It's useful to use decimal points for this division, too. So, 683 is the same as 683.0. The easiest way to divide by 100, is to move the numbers two places right. To divide by 1 000, move the numbers three places right.

$$683 \div 100$$

$$683.0 \div 100 = 6.83$$

The numbers have moved two places to the right.

Now try these  $47 \div 10$ $1\,245 \div 100$ $1\,711 \div 1\,000$

When writing remainders it is useful to remember these simple fractions ...

Long division

This is easy as long as the brain is fully engaged! Here goes with the standard method:

Infinity is anything that goes on for ever – such as a reflection of a reflection.

Warning!

Be careful if you are ever asked to divide a number or amount by zero. You could add millions and millions of zeros together and you still wouldn't get to one, so there must be a never-ending amount of zeros in any number. Any number divided by zero is infinity.

How many 24s in 6? None at all.

How many 24s in 65? 2 with 17 left over.

How many 24s in 173? 7 with 5 left over.

$$0\ 2\ 7\ r\ 5$$

$$24\ \overline{)\ 653}$$

Because the calculation works down the page, you have to move the 3 down when you need it.

You can use paper and pencil to work out 2 x 24 = 48. The answer goes here.

$$-\ 48$$

65 – 48 = 17, which is the remainder.

$$173$$

You have to put the 3 next to the 17 because you still need to deal with it.

How many 24s in 173? 7 x 24 is 168, so the answer is 7 with 5 left over.

You will probably need to use pencil and paper to work out 7 x 24 = 168.

$$-\ 168$$

173 – 168 = 5, which is the remainder.

$$5$$

This is the remainder.

The answer is

$$27\ r\ 5 \quad \text{or} \quad 27\tfrac{5}{24}$$

Carol's tips

"Giving remainders as answers is not very useful. It is better to give answers as fractions or decimals. To give the answer with a fraction, just put the remainder over whatever you have divided by.
Example:
$7 \div 3 = 2\ r\ 1$
$2\ r\ 1 = 2\tfrac{1}{3}$
$19 \div 4 = 4\ r\ 3$
$4\ r\ 3 = 4\tfrac{3}{4}$"

Now try these

$$18\ \overline{)\ 417} \qquad 23\ \overline{)\ 481} \qquad 36\ \overline{)\ 845}$$

... and the decimals that go with them: ½ = 0.5, ¼ = 0.25, ⅓ = 0.3333.

Times tables

People say you have to practise times tables to learn them – and that's true. But you may already know more than you think.

> **7 × 3 = 21**
> **3 × 7 = 21**

2 x 2 = 4	3 x 3 = 9	4 x 4 = 16	5 x 5 = 25	6 x 6 = 36	7 x 7 = 49	8 x 8 = 64	9 x 9 = 81
3 x 2 = 6	4 x 3 = 12	5 x 4 = 20	6 x 5 = 30	7 x 6 = 42	8 x 7 = 56	9 x 8 = 72	
4 x 2 = 8	5 x 3 = 15	6 x 4 = 24	7 x 5 = 35	8 x 6 = 48	9 x 7 = 63		
5 x 2 = 10	6 x 3 = 18	7 x 4 = 28	8 x 5 = 40	9 x 6 = 54			
6 x 2 = 12	7 x 3 = 21	8 x 4 = 32	9 x 5 = 45				
7 x 2 = 14	8 x 3 = 24	9 x 4 = 36					
8 x 2 = 16	9 x 3 = 27						
9 x 2 = 18							

Patterns in tables

An important thing to understand about times tables is that if you know one you also know the reverse. So, if you know that 7 x 3 = 21, you also know that 3 x 7 = 21. This means that even if you know only the 2 and 3 times tables you also know parts of the 4, 5, 6, 7, 8, and 9 times tables. This can help a lot, because if you take off the 1 and the 10 times tables, which are easy, the tables on the left are all you need to learn.

On target

A good way to practise times tables is by playing a game called target numbers. The game is very simple. Get a friend to write down a number between 1 and 100. Then try and think of number pairs that multiply together to make that number. You can use the chart at the back of this book to check your answers, but don't look until you have finished!

For example, the pairs that make **24** are **1 × 24, 2 × 12, 3 × 8, 4 × 6**

Two of a kind

You can use what you know in the 2, 3, 4, 5, and 10 times tables to work out the other ones you may have trouble with. If you know 2 x 5 is 10, then it's easy to work out 4 x 5 because it will be double. So 4 x 5 will be 20.

> **4 × 5**

2 × 5 = 10   **4 × 5 = 20**

Now try these

6 × 7

4 × 9

8 × 5

6 × 8

You can never practise your times tables enough.

Using what you already know

If you already know the 5 and 10 times tables, this will help you to work out the 4, 6, and 9 times tables.

If you need to work out 4 of a number, say 4 x 8, remember that

5 x 8 = 40

Then just take away one lot of 8:

40 – 8 = 32

If you need to work out 6 of a number, say 6 x 7, remember that

5 x 7 = 35

Then just add on one lot of 7:

35 + 7 = 42

If you need to work out 9 of a number, say 9 x 9, remember that

10 x 9 = 90

Then just take away one lot of 9:

90 – 9 = 81

Larger numbers

You may not believe it, but tables such as the 13 and 14 times tables are fairly easy if you work them out like this:

First work out 8 x 10 = 80. Easy.

8 X 10 = 80

8 X 3 = 24

104

Then work out 8 x 3 = 24. Easy.

Then add them together: 80 + 24 = 104. Easy!

First work out 7 x 10 = 70. Easy.

7 X 10 = 70

7 X 4 = 28

98

Then work out 7 x 4 = 28. Easy.

Then add them together: 70 + 28 = 98. Easy!

Now try these   6 x 13   9 x 14   7 x 15   4 x 19

Don't get stuck

If you are stuck on a times table, try going to the nearest one you do know. When you're as close as possible, either add or subtract until you reach the right amount. If you don't know 6 x 8, try using what you know of the 5 times table to help.

6 X 8

You probably know 5 x 8 = 40

5 x 8 = 40

So just add another 8 to make 48, which is the same as 6 x 8.

40 + 8 = 48

Carol's tips

Some times tables are harder to remember than others. 7 x 8 = 56 is a hard one. Remember the sum like this: 56 = 7 x 8. The numbers go in order: 5 6 7 8.

Use the tables you do know to help work out the ones you don't know.

Special numbers

9

You would think that numbers could never surprise you. But just when you least expect it they do the strangest things, even when you are doing times tables.

1 × 9	**= 09**
2 × 9	**= 18**
3 × 9	**= 27**
4 × 9	**= 36**
5 × 9	**= 45**
6 × 9	**= 54**
7 × 9	**= 63**
8 × 9	**= 72**
9 × 9	**= 81**
10 × 9	**= 90**

All the nines
Look at the times tables list on the left. Do you notice anything about the answers?

The first number in the answer goes up one at a time.

The second number goes down one at a time.

The first number in the answer is always one less than the number you are multiplying by.

The two numbers in the answer always add up to 9.

3 + 6 = 9

4 × 9 = 36

6 × 9

You can use the quirky nature of the nine times table to work out the answer when you don't know it off by heart. Here's how, using 6 x 9 as an example.

You know that the first number in your answer will be one less than 6 – that's 5.

6 × 9 = 5?

You also know the two digits in the answer add up to 9. What added to 5 makes 9? That's 4. So the answer is 54.

6 × 9 = 54

> **Now try these** 3 × 9   7 × 9   8 × 9   9 × 9

Factors
The numbers that multiply together to make a larger number are called its factors.

For example, the factors of **6** are **1, 2, 3,** and **6** because **1 × 6 = 6** and **2 × 3 = 6**

The factors of **18** are **1, 2, 3, 6, 9,** and **18** because **1 × 18 = 18, 2 × 9 = 18,** and **3 × 6 = 18**

> **Find the factors of these** 16 20 28 32

Carol's tips
" Because 1 goes into every whole number, and a number will always go into itself, every number has at least two factors: 1 and the number itself. Make sure you always include them in your list. "

Every number has at least two factors.

Prime numbers

Look at the number chart on the right. Some of the numbers are on blue squares. Can you see anything special about these numbers? When you investigate how many factors each "blue" number has, you will see that there are only two – 1 and the number itself. These special numbers are called prime numbers. One is not usually counted as a prime number.

What's so special about the blue numbers?

What's different about the green numbers?

The purple numbers are called perfect. Can you work out why?

1	2	3	4	5	6	7	8	9	10
11	12	13	14	15	16	17	18	19	20
21	22	23	24	25	26	27	28	29	30
31	32	33	34	35	36	37	38	39	40
41	42	43	44	45	46	47	48	49	50
51	52	53	54	55	56	57	58	59	60
61	62	63	64	65	66	67	68	69	70
71	72	73	74	75	76	77	78	79	80
81	82	83	84	85	86	87	88	89	90
91	92	93	94	95	96	97	98	99	100

Carol's tips
"The number 2 is the smallest prime number and the only one divisible by 2. This means that all prime numbers apart from 2 are odd numbers."

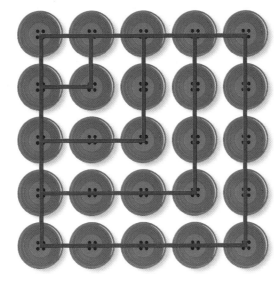

Square numbers

Look at the number chart again. Some numbers are on green squares. Can you see what is different about these numbers? They are called square numbers. This is because if you had the same number of counters, or buttons, they would make a square shape. The buttons on the left show the shape of square numbers.

Perfect numbers

You will see that there are two purple squares on the number chart. These are perfect numbers and are extra special. If you add the factors of a perfect number together (including 1, but not the number itself) the answer is the number itself.

For example: **1 + 2 + 3 = 6** and
1 + 2 + 4 + 7 + 14 = 28

The next perfect number after
28 is **496**

The largest known prime number has over 65 000 digits!

Carol's fun challenges ?

Lots of maths can be fun if you look at it as if it were a mystery waiting to be solved. Have a go at these puzzles and treat them as a challenge – not a problem.

Draw the circles in ink and use a pencil for the numbers so that you can erase them and try again if they don't work.

Total 15

This is a famous maths problem that has a history going back hundreds of years. The idea is very simple. Copy out the drawing on the right. Write the numbers 1-9 in the circles, but position them so that each of the rows – including the diagonals – add up to a total of 15.

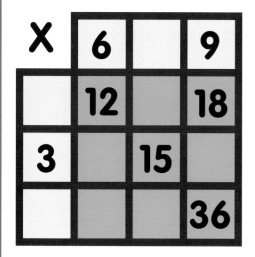

Missing multipliers

This table is part of a multiplication table like the one at the back of this book, but some numbers are missing. Copy the table and try to complete it.

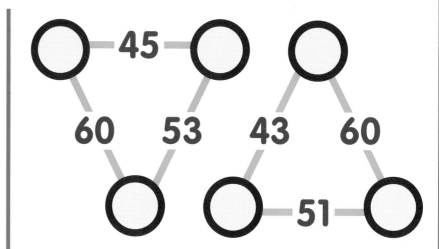

Find the corners

Copy the number triangles above. Put a number in each of the circles so that by adding the numbers in the circles on each line, you make the number in the middle of each line.

Totals, differences, and products

This set of questions will make you think hard about numbers – you will have to think whether to add, subtract, multiply, or any combination of the three.

Find two numbers which total **9** and give a product of **20**.

Which two numbers have a product of **21** and a difference of **4**?

Two numbers have a total of **35** but have a difference of **7**. What are the two numbers?

The product of two numbers is **63** and the difference between them is **2**. What are the numbers?

The product is the answer you get when you multiply two or more numbers together.

In your head

Try this without using pencil and paper or a calculator. Start with 1, double it, add 7, multiply by 6, subtract 20, halve that number, add the number of days in a week, divide by 6, add the number of minutes in an hour. What number multiplied by itself makes that number?

How many squares?

Look at the pencils on the left. How many squares do the pencils make? Be careful! The answer is not 9.

Get in sequence

A sequence is a series of numbers that are connected in some way. The trick is to spot how they are connected and then be able to continue the sequence. Try to continue each of these sequences.

17 9 1 ? ? ?

4 000 2 000 1 000 ? ?

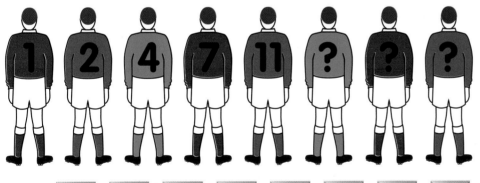

3 5 9 17 33 ? ? ?

1 1 2 3 5 8 ? ? ?

Not so simple

These sequences will probably make you think a bit more. They might involve doing more than just one calculation at a time. You may have to multiply and then subtract or work out some other cunning method!

General knowledge

These sequences are definitely tricky and you will need to use your general knowledge as much as mathematics.

1 2 5 10 20 ? ? ?

31 28 31 30 ? ? ? ?

Number sequences do not always have a purely mathematical solution.

Algebra & Brackets

Scary? No! Algebra might sound a bit tricky but it's actually a lot of fun and is really to do with solving puzzles. In algebra, a letter or sign represents the thing you have to find out. The letter X is often used but any letter or symbol will do.

Symbolic sum

In the example on the right, a different symbol is used instead of the one that you are used to. Do you have any idea what the mystery symbol stands for? In this case it's a minus sign: 11 − 3 = 8.

$$11 * 3 = 8$$

Now try these $10 * 6 = 60$ $24 * 9 = 15$ $32 * 4 = 8$

Mystery letters

In algebra an X is often used to represent an unknown number or amount. The mathematician has to solve the problem and work out what the X stands for.

Here is a simple example. Three model cars cost 90p, how much does each car cost?

We replace the cost of each car with X the unknown.

$$3X = 90$$

Now we have to divide by three to find the value of one X.

Divide both sides by 3.

$$X = 30$$

3X divided by 3 is X.

90 divided by 3 is 30. So one car costs 30p.

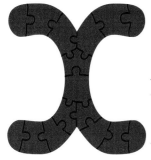

Now try these
1. Jamie thinks of a number – X – and then doubles it. The result is **28**. What was Jamie's number?
2. Four lots of X are **36**. What is X?
3. You add X to **9** and end up with **13**. What is X?

X is the same as 1X.

Solving equations

In working out the value of X, you are actually solving an equation. An equation may sound hard but it is simply a mathematical statement where two parts are the same – as shown by the equals sign. Take a look at how to solve the equation 4X = 20, and then work out the others for yourself.

$$4X = 20$$

This means that 4 lots of something are the same as 20.

It is not too difficult to work out that the mystery number is 5 because 4 lots of 5 are 20.

Carol's tips
66 Algebra and equations may appear quite complicated but you will be surprised how well you can do just by applying common sense. 99

5 + 5 + 5 + 5 =  20

Now try these $7X = 63$ $19 + X = 50$ $X - 12 = 8$

Same sum, different answers!

If you try to work this sum out you could get confused. If you start by working out 4 x 3 and then add 5, the answer is 17. On the other hand, if you first add the 3 and the 5 to get 8 and then multiply that by 4, you get 32. Neither answer is wrong. To help stop this confusion mathematicians use brackets.

$$4 \times 3 + 5 = ?$$

Let's look at the sum again, this time using brackets.

Multiply 4 by 3 to get 12.

$$(4 \times 3) + 5 = 17$$

Then add 5.   *The answer is 17.*

Brackets

Mathematicians put brackets around the bits that have to be done first, so that you know where to start when you are doing complicated sums.

Add 3 and 5 to get 8.

$$4 \times (3 + 5) = 32$$

Then multiply by 4.   *The answer is 32.*

Now try these

$$6 + (4 \times 3) = \qquad (6 + 4) \times 3 =$$

$$12 \div (4 + 2) = \qquad (12 \div 4) + 2 =$$

Remember the brackets surround the bits that have to be done first. $(2 + 3) \times 5 = $ **25**

Perimeter & Area

Perimeter just means the distance around the edge of something. In real life this usually means things like the perimeter of your bedroom when your parents are buying new wallpaper.

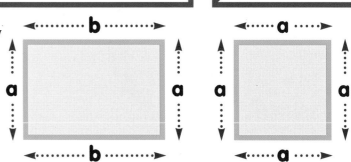

A trundle wheel measures long distances.

Perimeters

Most of the time perimeters only need to be worked out fairly roughly. A room will probably need to be measured to the nearest centimetre using a simple tape measure. Perimeters of larger amounts can be measured using more technical equipment.

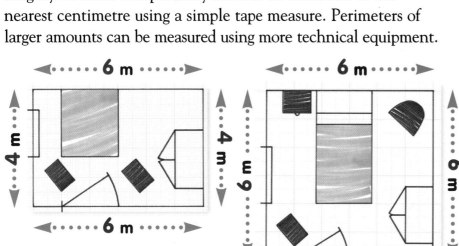

Calculating perimeter

The easiest place to start is with simple shapes like rectangles and squares. The perimeter of the rectangle on the far left will be: 6 m + 4 m + 6 m + 4 m = 20 m. The perimeter of the square on the left will be: 6 m + 6 m + 6 m + 6 m = 24 m.

Formulas

Mathematicians like to have a general way of writing rules. These are called formulas and usually involve using letters instead of numbers.

Perimeter = P

The measurements on the rectangle on the right have been replaced by "a" and "b". The perimeter will be a + b + a + b, which is 2a + 2b. The formula for the perimeter of a square is even easier. Look at the square on the far right. The perimeter will be a + a + a + a, which is 4a.

> **P = 2a + 2b**

> **P = 4a**

> **Now work out these** The perimeter of a room that is **2.5 m** by **3.2 m**.
> The perimeter of a garden that is **15 m** by **12 m**.

The perimeter is the distance around the edge of something.

Area

Although the perimeters of shapes can usually be found fairly easily, finding area is more difficult. Area is the space inside a shape, and working it out can involve some maths that definitely isn't easy! For now we'll look at simpler shapes.

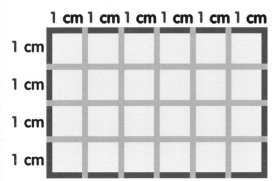

1 cm 1 cm 1 cm 1 cm 1 cm 1 cm
1 cm
1 cm
1 cm
1 cm

Calculating area

You measure areas by imagining the shape to

$$4 \times 6 = 24 \text{ cm}^2$$

be full of squares. The easiest units to use are centimetre squares, although you can use millimetres, metres, and other units as well. The way to find the area of these shapes is to multiply one side by the other. The area of the rectangle on the left will be 24 squares because there are 4 rows of 6.

Area = A

The formula for the area of a rectangle such as the one on the right is easy. The area is "a" multiplied by "b", so the formula is A = ab. The area of a square is also found by multiplying one side by the other but, because it's a square, the sides are the same length. The formula is A = a x a, which is written as a².

$$A = a \times b \text{ or } A = ab$$

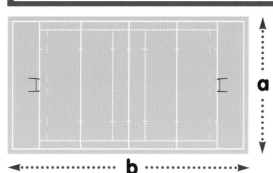
a
b

$$A = a^2$$

a
a

Now try these
What is the area of a rectangular field that is **40 m** by **60 m?**
What is the area of a book cover that is **11 cm** by **15 cm?**

7
3
2
6
1
1

4
3
1 2
6
2

6
1
3
5
6
3

To work out these areas, just split the shapes into simple rectangles and carry on as before.

Complex shapes

Unfortunately, not all shapes are as simple as squares and rectangles. The hardest you might come across for now are complex shapes. Complex shapes are just rectangles or squares joined together in different ways.

Area is the space inside a shape.

Ratio & Proportion

Ratio is a mathematical idea that is very similar to fractions. Ratio means one thing compared with another. Proportion is another way of expressing a similar idea.

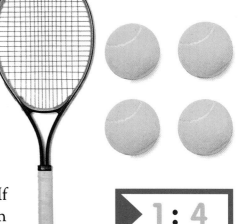

Ratios

A tennis team has one tennis racket for every four tennis balls. The important mathematical part of this sentence is "for every". If you know how many balls the team have for every racket, you can work out how many they would have if they had four rackets: 16.

 1 : 4

Writing ratios
In maths we have a special way of writing ratio. We use two little dots like these :

1 : 5

If the ratio is one for every five we would write 1 : 5.

Now try these
What would you write if the ratio is:
One for every 10?   Two for every 15?
One for every 20?   Three for every 11?

Ratio and food
The idea of ratio is often used in connection with recipes. If a recipe has enough ingredients for one person, what happens if you want to make the same food for three people? For every item you would have to use three times as much – that's a ratio of 1 to 3.

1 : 3

If the ratio is one for every three we would write 1 : 3.

Ratio and shapes
Looking at shapes divided into sections helps to visualize ratios. Look at the shape on the right. There is one blue section for every three green sections. The ratio of blue to green is 1 : 3

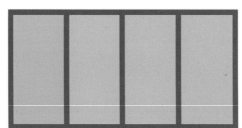

Warning!
You have to be careful to write ratios the right way round. What is the ratio of green for every blue in the diagram on the left? It isn't 1 : 3. It will be 3 : 1.

Now try these
What is the ratio of green to blue in each shape?

28 : 56 = ½

The : sign means "for every".

Ratio and fractions

The connection between ratios and fractions is fairly simple. Here is an example. You could say that 5 in every 7 days are school days. The ratio is 5 : 7. The fraction is ⅝. Or you could say that 2 days in every 7 are the weekend. The ratio is 2 : 7. The fraction is ⅖.

> 5 : 7

Now try these

Write each of these ratios as a fraction.

4 : 5   3 : 10   4 : 7   8 : 12

Carol's tips

" Sometimes ratios can be less complicated than they appear. Look at this shape.

The ratio of green to blue is 4 : 6 or ⅘, but ⅘ is the same as – equivalent to – ⅔. So 4 : 6 is the same as 2 : 3. "

Proportion

Proportion is another way of expressing a ratio or a fraction. Look at this example. There are 28 gems below, eight are yellow, 20 are blue. What proportion of the gems are yellow? The proportion is eight in every 28, which is the same as 8 : 28, which is the same as ⁸⁄₂₈ or ²⁄₇! Now look at the swimmers on the right and answer the questions below.

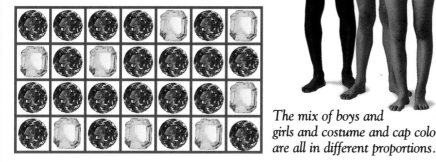

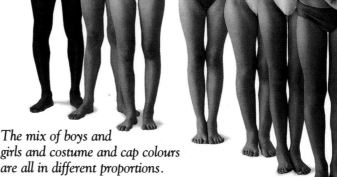

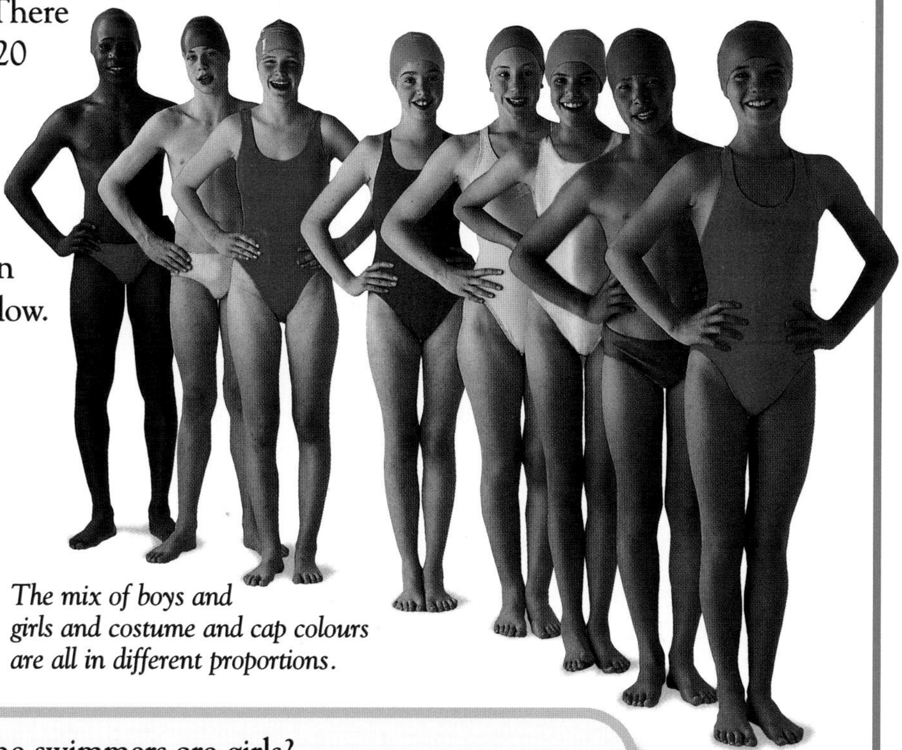

The mix of boys and girls and costume and cap colours are all in different proportions.

Now try these

What proportion of the swimmers are girls?
What proportion of the swimmers are wearing yellow costumes?
What proportion of the swimmers are wearing blue caps?

And finally!

Percentages are linked to ratios, fractions, and proportions. Bearing this in mind can you answer the percentage question on the right?

Now try these

1. In a class of children the proportion of boys to girls is 2 in every 3. If there are 12 boys, how many children are there in the class?
2. In a box of assorted chocolates, 40% of the chocolates are plain and the rest are milk. What ratio are the milk to plain?

Ratios, fractions, proportion, and percentages are all closely linked.

2 : 58 = 1 : 29

Fractions

Just as numbers can become larger and larger, they can also become smaller and smaller. One way we show numbers that are divided into pieces smaller than 1 is by using fractions.

Simple fractions

$\frac{1}{2}$ **of** 20

Fractions are written as one number over another, like this: ½. This tells you that one "thing" is being divided into two. The "thing" can be a number, a shape, or an amount. To work out a problem with fractions, you divide by the amount on the bottom of the fraction. Look at the example on the right to see how to work out half of 20.

Let's find out what is half of 20.

Divide 20 by the number at the bottom of the fraction.

20 divided by 2 is 10

$$\frac{1}{2} \text{ of } 20 = 10$$

So half of 20 is 10.

Now try these

$\frac{1}{3}$ of **24** $\frac{1}{5}$ of **30**

$\frac{1}{10}$ of **90** $\frac{1}{4}$ of **28**

Carol's tips

❝When simplifying a fraction, the first thing to do is to see if both numbers are even. If they are, you know that 2 will divide into both of them.❞

Get simple

$\frac{3}{6} = \frac{1}{2}$

Look at the two cakes on the right. Half of each cake has been outlined, but the cake on the left has three slices out of six marked. We write three out of six as ⅜, but it is possible to simplify this into ½. To simplify fractions you have to find a number that divides into both numbers.

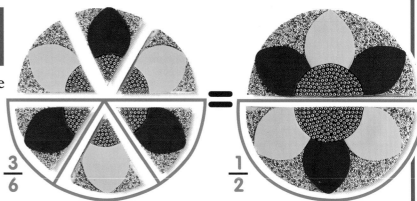

$\frac{3}{6}$ $=$ $\frac{1}{2}$

Try to simplify these

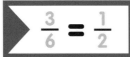

$\frac{4}{8}$ $\frac{6}{15}$ $\frac{5}{20}$ $\frac{10}{50}$

3 into 3 goes once.

3 into 6 goes twice.

$$\frac{3 \div 3 = 1}{6 \div 3 = 2}$$

Instead of writing ⅜ we can write ½. This is called cancelling.

Fractions often come in large families. It helps to get to know them:

Complicated fractions

Fractions don't always come in the simple variety with a one on the top, but this needn't worry you! Here's what to do when you come across more complicated-looking fractions like ⅗.

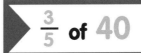

$\frac{3}{5}$ of 40

To find ⅗ of 40, start by finding ⅕ and then multiply by 3 – that's all there is to it!

Divide 40 by 5.

$\frac{1}{5}$ of **40 = 8** — *40 divided by 5 is 8.*

If ⅕ is 8, multiply by 3 to find out what ⅗ are.

3 × 8 = 24 — *3 times 8 is 24.*

$\frac{3}{5}$ of **40 = 24** — *So ⅗ of 40 is 24.*

> **Carol's tips**
> "Always look for the largest number that divides into the top and bottom numbers of a fraction. For example ¹²⁄₃₆ can be divided by 2 or 4, but if you notice that it can also be divided by 12, you can turn ¹²⁄₃₆ into ⅓ straight away!"

Now try these $\frac{5}{7}$ of **21** $\frac{4}{9}$ of **36** $\frac{3}{4}$ of **24** $\frac{4}{5}$ of **30**

Improper fractions

$\frac{5}{2} = 2\frac{1}{2}$

Fractions will usually have a smaller number on the top than on the bottom. But sometimes the number on the top is bigger than the one on the bottom. Mathematicians don't like that sort of thing, so they make it look better – not so improper. For example ⁵⁄₂ is an improper fraction, but it can be "properly" written as 2½. All you do is divide the top number by the bottom number.

⁵⁄₂ means the same as 5 halves.

2 divides into 5 2½ times.

4 half bottles contain the same as 2 whole ones, so we can use those 4 halves to make 2 whole ones and just tag the spare ½ on the end.

Now try these $\frac{14}{3}$ $\frac{12}{5}$ $\frac{16}{6}$ $\frac{13}{2}$ $\frac{7}{2}$ $\frac{11}{4}$ $\frac{19}{3}$

Cancelling in reverse

$\frac{1}{2} = \frac{5}{10}$

Fractions can be made simpler by cancelling, but you can reverse this process. Take a look at the calculation on the right to find out how many tenths are the same as a half. The golden rule for this calculation is always do the same to the top number as you do to the bottom number.

Multiply the top of the fraction by 5.   **1 ······ × 5 = 5**

2 ······ × 5 = 10

Multiply the bottom of the fraction by 5. The answer will have 10 at the bottom.   *½ is equivalent to ⁵⁄₁₀.*

Decimals

The decimal system is a number system based on 10. We write decimals with a dot called a decimal point. Decimals are often used for money and measurement.

Decimals in money

In everyday life we mainly use decimals in connection with money. If you had a few pounds and some spare change in your pocket, you could write down the exact amount of money as a decimal.

£8.95

For example if you had 8 pounds and 95 pence, you would write £8.95.

In maths, £8.95 really means 8 whole pounds and 95 hundredths.

Calculating money

Calculators are very useful but can be a bit tricky, especially when you are doing calculations involving money. Don't forget the decimal point when you enter amounts of money on a calculator.

2.5

An amount such as £2.50 will appear as 2.5, which does not exist as money. It has to be 2.50, so be careful.

0.54

Unless you enter the decimal point, 54p will appear as 54, which means £54. It needs to be entered as .54 because it is 54 hundredths of a pound.

Smaller and smaller

The further numbers go to the right of the decimal point, the smaller they become.

0.1
0.01
0.001
0.0001
0.00001

With each step to the right, this number gets 10 times smaller.

Rounding up and down

To keep things simple, we often "round" a decimal number up or down to the nearest whole number. If you need to round .5, you always round up.

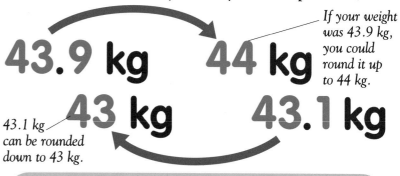

43.9 kg   **44 kg**

If your weight was 43.9 kg, you could round it up to 44 kg.

43 kg   **43.1 kg**

43.1 kg can be rounded down to 43 kg.

Now try rounding these
155.6 cm   7.1 kg   99.5 grams

Decimals and fractions

There is a strong connection between decimals and fractions. If you have a box of 10 paints, one paint would be 1/10 of the contents. You would write this as 0.1 in decimals.

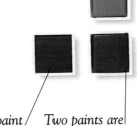

One paint is 1/10 or 0.1. Two paints are 2/10 = 1/5 or 0.2.

The 10 paints in the box can be broken down into fractions or decimals.

Decimals into fractions

It's easy to change decimals into fractions. Let's take 0.5 as an example. Don't panic. Take it a step at a time.

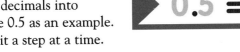

> 0.5 = $\frac{1}{2}$

First draw a line under the decimal. This is called the fraction line.

Put a 1 under the line.

Then add one 0 for each figure to the right of the decimal point above.

Cross out the 0 and the decimal point.

$$\frac{0.5}{10} = \frac{5}{10} = \frac{1}{2}$$

You add the 1 and the 0 because decimals are made up of units of 10.

If you know your fraction equivalents, you'll know that 5/10 is the same as 1/2.

Now change these into fractions   0.72   0.45   0.64   0.8   0.35

Fractions into decimals

Before changing a fraction into a decimal, you must realize that a fraction is a division sum in disguise. For instance, 1/2 really means: "How many 2s are there in 1?" To change 1/2 into a decimal, set up the sum as follows:

> $\frac{1}{2}$ = 0.5

There are 5 2s in 10, so the answer is 0.5.

We know that 2 into 1 doesn't go.

Put a 0 above the line followed by a decimal point

Divide 2 into 10 and put the answer above the line.

Add a 0 to the 1 to show that you're working with decimals.

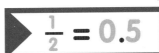

Put a decimal point below the line, too, and carry the 1 over the decimal point.

Now change these into decimals $\frac{1}{5}$ $\frac{2}{5}$ $\frac{1}{4}$ $\frac{3}{4}$ $\frac{4}{5}$ $\frac{3}{10}$ $\frac{7}{10}$ $\frac{4}{8}$ $\frac{3}{5}$

You can change any fraction into a decimal.

Percentages

Percentage is a way of describing numbers or amounts of things as part of 100, even when they aren't.

Percentages and fractions

If you had 4 boxes and half of them were blue, you could say that 50% (fifty percent) of your boxes were blue. There is a strong link between percentages and fractions. 50% means $^{50}/_{100}$, which is the same as ½. So if ½ of the boxes are blue that means two of them.

$$50\% = \tfrac{1}{2}$$

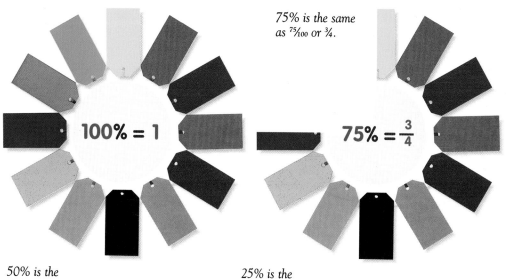

75% is the same as $^{75}/_{100}$ or ¾.

$$100\% = 1$$

$$75\% = \tfrac{3}{4}$$

50% is the same as $^{50}/_{100}$ or ½.

25% is the same as $^{25}/_{100}$ or ¼.

$$50\% = \tfrac{1}{2}$$

$$25\% = \tfrac{1}{4}$$

Carol's tips

" Here are some more common percentages and their fraction equivalents that you should try to remember:

$20\% = {}^{20}/_{100} = \tfrac{1}{5}$

$10\% = {}^{10}/_{100} = \tfrac{1}{10}$

$12.5\% = \tfrac{1}{8}$

$33.33\% = \tfrac{1}{3}$ "

Common percentages

Calculations are often easier if you think of percentages as fractions and try to visualize them as part of a whole. Try to memorize the most common percentages.

Easy money

It is easy to work out percentages with money and length because there are 100 pennies in a pound and 100 centimetres in a metre. For instance, 1% of £1.00 is 1p and 1% of 1 metre is 1 cm. If you are asked what 67% of £1.00 is, it's easy – 67p!

Now try these
What is 43% of £1.00?
How long is 93% of 1 metre?
How much is 37% of £1.00?
What is 84% of 1 metre?

Percentages and fractions are closely linked.

Get your skates on

A typical percentage problem will look like this. A pair of inline skates that usually sells for £15.00 has 20% knocked off its price in a sale. What is the sale price? To work this out you have to find 20% of £15.00. When you say "of" in this kind of sum it means multiply, so the sum you are really working out is 20% x 15.

20% of £15

First remember that 20% is the same as ²⁰⁄₁₀₀.

You can simplify ²⁰⁄₁₀₀ to ⅕.

$$20\% = \frac{20}{100} = \frac{1}{5}$$

20% has changed into a fraction.

To work out ⅕ of 15 divide 15 by 5.

$$\frac{1}{5} \text{ of } 15 = 15 \div 5 = 3$$

⅕ of 15 is 3.

Subtract £3 from the full price to work out the sale price.

$$£15 - £3 = £12$$

The sale price is £12.

Now try this
A bottle usually contains 600 ml of juice, but for a short while has an extra 20% free. How much is in the special bottle?

Percentage problem

Percentage problems are sometimes phrased in another way. For example, what percentage of 40 is 8? To work this out, you have to make a fraction out of the 8 and the 40 and then multiply by 100 to turn the fraction into a percentage.

20% of 40

First, make a fraction out of the numbers. Then multiply the 8 by 100.

8 multiplied by 100 is 800.

$$\frac{8}{40} \times 100 = \frac{800}{40}$$

Divide 800 by 40. This can be done with a calculator if you don't want to tackle the division.

$$\frac{800}{40} = 20$$

800 divided by 40 is 20.

So 8 is 20% of 40.

Decimal links
Try to remember this table, which shows the links between some percentages, fractions, and decimals.

Percentage	Fraction	Decimal
50%	$\frac{1}{2}$	0.5
25%	$\frac{1}{4}$	0.25
75%	$\frac{3}{4}$	0.75
10%	$\frac{1}{10}$	0.1

Now try these
What percentage of 60 is 12?
What percentage of 30 is 15?
What percentage of 10 is 9?

Percentages and decimals are closely linked, too.

70% of 50 = 35

Squares & Cubes

A square number is the result of multiplying a number by itself. In other words 9 is an example of a square number because it is the result of multiplying 3 by 3. You have to multiply a number by itself three times to get a cube number.

Square numbers

If you multiply 7 by 7 the answer is 49, so 49 is a square number. If you want to create a square number you don't have to write 7 x 7 or whatever the numbers are. You can use a special sign, which is a small 2 up in the air alongside the number, like these: 3^2 or 7^2.

$$7 \times 7 = 7^2$$

Warning!

Remember that the small 2 does not mean multiply by 2. The small 2 means multiply the number by itself.

Squares with numbers

It's useful to think of square numbers as actual square shapes. Each of the squares on the right is made up of rows and columns. You can see that square numbers have the same numbers of rows as they do columns.

$2^2 = 4$

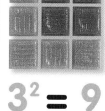

$3^2 = 9$

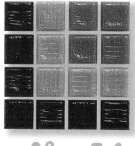

$4^2 = 16$

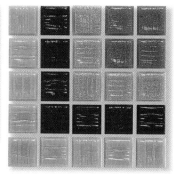

$5^2 = 25$

Areas of squares

Square numbers are used when working out the area of squares! The area of the garden on the right is 8 m by 8 m or 64 m².

$$64 \text{ m}^2$$

Multiply the length of the two sides to find the area.

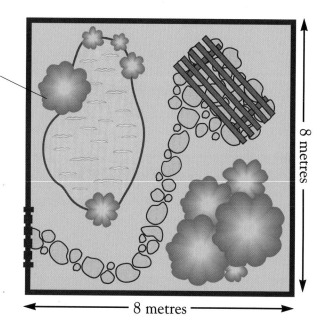

8 metres

8 metres

Now work out these

$15^2 \quad 13^2 \quad 12^2 \quad 7^2$

12 m x 12 m	10 cm x 10 cm
15 m x 15 m	6 cm x 6 cm

Try to visualize square numbers as actual square shapes.

Sign of the times

Mathematicians don't like wasting time – or words – so they have a special sign to say, "What number multiplied by itself gives a certain number?" It is called the square root sign.

This is the square root sign.

$$\sqrt{36}$$

This sign means, "What is the square root of 36?" or, "What number multiplied by itself results in 36?" The answer is 6, so 6 is the square root of 36.

Cube numbers

A cube number is the result of multiplying a

$$6 \times 6 \times 6 = 6^3$$

number by itself three times. We represent numbers to be cubed by using a small 3, so that 6 x 6 x 6 is written as 6^3, and the answer is 216. If square numbers are numbers that can be arranged into square shapes, you might think that cube numbers are numbers that can be arranged into cube shapes – and you would be right!

Warning!

The small 3 does not mean multiply by 3, it means multiply the number by itself three times.

Cubes with numbers

You will notice from the pictures below that a cube number can be found by multiplying the number of balls in a row by the number of balls in a column by the number of balls in the depth.

$$2 \times 2 \times 2 = 8$$

$$3 \times 3 \times 3 = 27$$

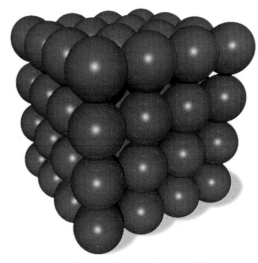

$$4 \times 4 \times 4 = 64$$

Now try these 10^3 8^3 1^3 15^3 7^3 11^3

Cubes and volume

We measure the volume of objects in cubic measures – often cubic centimetres. A cubic centimetre is about the size of a sugar cube and is 1cm by 1cm by 1cm. Volume is the amount of space in three dimensions, so to find the volume of a shape we multiply the length by the width by the height.

$$125 \text{ cm}^3$$

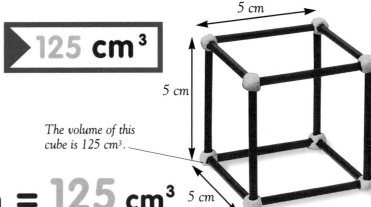

The volume of this cube is 125 cm³.

5 cm

5 cm

5 cm

$$5 \text{ cm} \times 5 \text{ cm} \times 5 \text{ cm} = 125 \text{ cm}^3$$

Volume is the amount of space in three dimensions.

$$\sqrt{1369} = 37$$

Negative numbers

Be positive about negative numbers! Negative numbers sound a bit nasty but they're just an extension of the number line, which you have probably used before to help with simple sums.

The number line can extend for ever and ever in both directions.

-10 -9 -8 -7 -6 -5 -4 -3 -2 -1 0 1 2 3 4 5 6 7 8 9 10

Negative numbers   *Positive numbers*

Less than

Wherever you are on the number line, the numbers to the left are less than those on the right. In mathematics there is a special sign for less than.

The sign is this: **<**

Instead of saying 4 is less than 7, you can write:

$$4 < 7$$

Instead of saying –12 is less than –1 you can write:

$$-12 < -1$$

Greater than

Wherever you are on the number line, the numbers to the right are always greater than those on the left. There is another special sign for greater than.

The sign is this: **>**

Instead of writing 5 is greater than 2, you can write:

$$5 > 2$$

You can use this sign with negative numbers, too. Instead of saying –2 is greater than –5 you can write:

$$-2 > -5$$

Working with negative numbers

Working with negative numbers can be a little tricky, and it's useful to keep the number line in mind or even draw one quickly when you have problems to do.

$$6 - 8$$

If you start at the 6 on the number line and then move back 8 steps (because you are subtracting), you will end up at –2. So 6 – 8 is –2.

Now try these

4 – 9	–1 – 4
1 – 4	3 – 7
2 – 8	–5 – 5

Taking temperatures

You will most often see negative numbers being used on thermometers. They don't usually appear on thermometers you would use to measure your body temperature because if your temperature was negative – you'd be very, very dead! You usually find negative temperatures on thermometers that measure the warmth of the air, or rooms, or freezers.

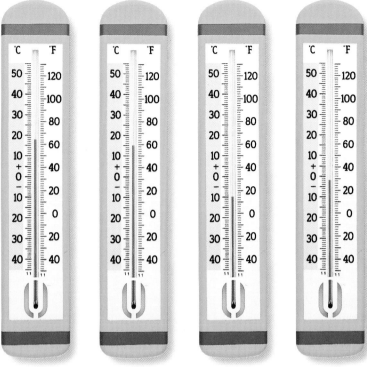

These thermometers are all showing different temperatures. Some are negative and some are positive.

Carol's tips
"You usually measure temperatures in degrees Celsius and write ° C for short."

Now try these
What Celsius temperature is shown on each thermometer?

What happens if all of the temperatures drop by 2° C?

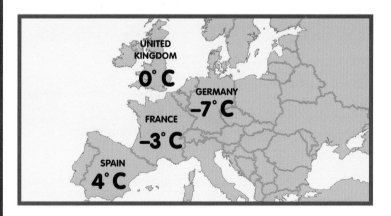

UNITED KINGDOM
0°C

GERMANY
-7°C

FRANCE
-3°C

SPAIN
4°C

Weather maps

Weather maps are another place where you often see negative numbers – especially in the winter!

Imagine the temperatures in each country shown on the map went up by 5° C. What would the new temperatures be?

Carol's tips
"Lots of people find it difficult to remember which way the arrow tip points for greater than and less than. Just remember that the arrow always points at the smaller number."

Now try these

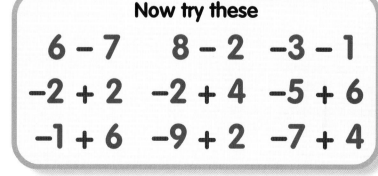

6 – 7   8 – 2   –3 – 1

–2 + 2   –2 + 4   –5 + 6

–1 + 6   –9 + 2   –7 + 4

On the number line, the numbers on the right are greater than those on the left.

Co-ordinates

You are hiking in the woods with friends when you realize that you are lost. You have a radio to call for help, but how do you explain your exact position on your map? You do it by giving numbers called co-ordinates.

Find your spot

To find your first co-ordinate on the map, run your finger along the numbered line at the bottom until it is directly under your location. This line is the x-axis, and the number your finger reaches is the x-co-ordinate. Next, run your finger up the numbered line at the side of the map. This line is the y-axis, and the number you read off is the y-co-ordinate.

Writing co-ordinates

We write down co-ordinates in brackets. The x-co-ordinate always comes first, followed by a comma and then the y-co-ordinate.

The co-ordinates of this location are (2, 3).

The co-ordinates of this location are (3, 1).

Carol's tips

"To remember which co-ordinate comes first, memorize this phrase: "along the passage and up the stairs"."

The four quadrants

The x-axis and y-axis on a map stop at 0. In fact the area, or quadrant (quarter), that you use on a map is just one of four. But in maths, co-ordinates can be negative numbers too. We can show them on a chart by extending the x-axis and y-axis past 0. The two lines divide the chart into four quadrants.

The lines no longer stop at 0 but extend downwards and across to continue the number lines in both directions.

The lines and numbers can extend as long as is needed for the problem.

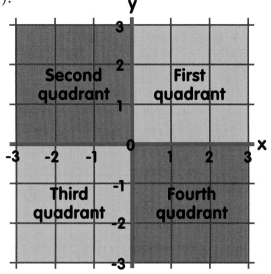

The x-co-ordinate is always written first.

Positions in quadrants

You can position places on the four quadrants in exactly the same way as you do on the more familiar single quadrant.

For example: On the chessboard on the right (–2, 2) will be 2 to the left of 0 and 2 upwards.

The position (–2, –3) will be –2, that's 2 to the left of 0, and 3 down.

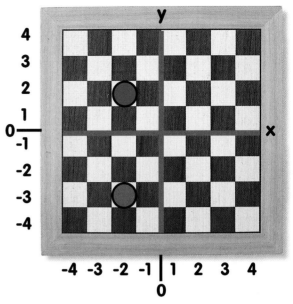

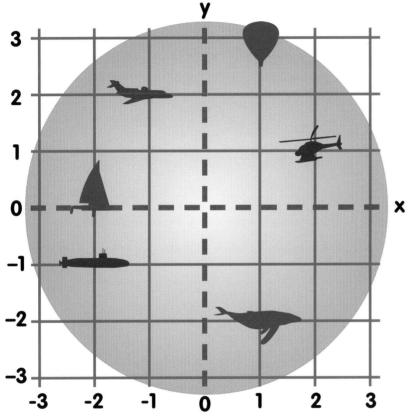

Carol's tips
"The "Along the passage and up the stairs," rule still works with the four quadrants, but it might not be up the stairs. It might be down to the cellar instead!"

Writing the positions

Try writing down the co-ordinates of the centre of the objects on the chart on the left. Remember to put them in brackets with a comma between each number.

Moving squares

Look at the diagram on the right. If the square slides four spaces to the right, what are the new co-ordinates of each corner? Now move the sloping shape two spaces to the left. What are the new co-ordinates of its corners? Be careful – some positions will change quadrant. Watch out for negative numbers becoming positive, and vice versa.

Now try these
Use a ruler to draw a chart like the one on the right, then mark on the following points:
A (2, 4); B (–4, 0); C (1, 5); D (–4, –4); E (0, 0)

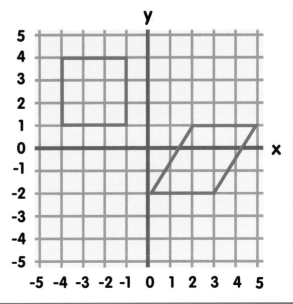

The y-co-ordinate is always written second.

Checking answers

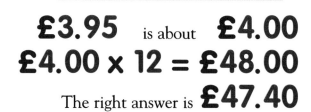

Sooner or later even the best mathematicians can make mistakes even when they are using calculators and computers. In maths you can use various ways of checking to see if you are correct.

Rounding

£3.95 × 12

Rounding up or down gives you an idea of what an answer should be. If you want to work out £3.95 x 12, you can round £3.95 up to £4.00 and then multiply by 12. The answer is £48.00. If you work out the original sum and your answer is nowhere near £48.00, you'll know that you have got it wrong.

£3.95 is about **£4.00**
£4.00 × 12 = £48.00
The right answer is **£47.40**

Now try these   **£5.08 × 14**   **286 × 9**   **712 ml × 19**

Working in reverse

One of the easiest ways to check answers is to go into reverse. Here's an example. Subtract 237 from 480 and then work backwards to see if your answer is correct.

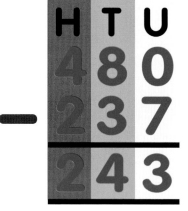

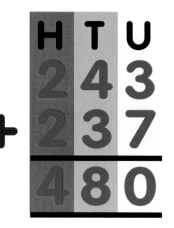

Carol's tips
" The reverse method also works with adding. For example if you add 378 to 469 and get an answer of 847, you can double check by taking 469 away from 847. Your answer should be 378. "

Try these, but be careful – one is wrong

252	563	805	726	176
-186	-292	-479	-447	-103
66	271	326	259	73

Different methods

Although everyone has a favourite way of working out a problem, you should know the different ways of coming to an answer. If you are not sure you have the right answer, or want to make absolutely certain you are correct, you can try different methods to do the same calculation. Here are some alternative ways of working out 17 x 14. First you can use the standard method on the right, then try splitting the numbers up (below), and finally check the answer by reversing.

17 x 14

This is the standard method of doing multiplication.

$$\begin{array}{r} 17 \\ \times\, 14 \\ \hline \end{array}$$

10 times 17 is 170. — **170**

4 times 17 is 68. — **68**

Finally add 170 and 68 together to get the answer 238. — **238**

Think of 14 as 10 and 4, and 17 as 10 and 7.

First multiply the **4** by **7**	**4 x 7 =**	**28**
Now multiply the **4** by **10**	**4 x 10 =**	**40**
Now multiply the **10** by **7**	**10 x 7 =**	**70**
Now multiply the **10** by **10**	**10 x 10 =**	**100**
Finally, add them all together		**= 238**

You can also use the reverse method to check the answer. If 238 is the correct answer, you should be able to divide it by 14 and get 17, or by 17 and get 14!

238 ÷ 14 = 17

You should be able to divide the answer by either of the original numbers to get the other original number.

238 ÷ 17 = 14

Now try these

156 x 26

263 x 47

648 x 59

174 x 75

Using a calculator

Many people use calculators to work out mathematical problems but that doesn't necessarily mean they get the right answer. It is so easy to press the wrong buttons or enter a wrong number. So, you should still use the reverse method to check answers.

Don't put your trust in calculators. You are much better off working out the calculation yourself.

Check these by reversing

2671 − 1453 = 1218

7452 − 6038 = 1414

6815 − 4051 = 2764

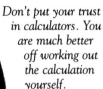

Always double check when using a calculator.

43 x 22 = 946 ÷ 22 = 43

Carol's maths tricks !

In this book there are lots of clever ways to make maths easy. Here are some of the most helpful hints. When you're in a tricky maths spot you can pull one of these out of the hat.

Doubles

Doubling numbers is usually fairly easy

> 34 + 34

> 47 + 47

as long as you take small steps that can be managed. The trick is to double the tens, then double the units, then add the answers together.

To double **34**, begin by doubling the **30**	30 x 2 = 60
Then double the **4**	4 x 2 = 8
Finally, add the answers together	= 68

It's a bit trickier when the numbers doubled are more than 5:

To double **47**, begin by doubling the **40**	40 x 2 = 80
Then double the **7**	7 x 2 = 14
Finally, add the answers together	= 94

Now double these

16	64
25	52
37	73
49	81

Halves

Halving works in a similar way to doubling. Begin by halving the tens, then halve the units, and then add the two answers together.

> 68 ÷ 2

> 76 ÷ 2

To halve **68**, begin by halving the **60**	60 ÷ 2 = 30
Then halve the **8**	8 ÷ 2 = 4
Finally, add the answers together	34

Here's an example that's a bit trickier:

To halve **76**, begin by halving the **70**	70 ÷ 2 = 35
Then halve the **6**	6 ÷ 2 = 3
Finally, add the answers together	38

Now halve these

42	24
78	84
36	92

If you add two even numbers together, the result is always an even number.

Partitions

You probably know lots more times tables than you think. Do you know what six 17s are? Just break the 17 into 10 and 7, multiply both by six and add the answers together. The proper mathematical word for breaking a number into bits is partitioning.

> **6 × 17**

Begin by multiplying the **10**	$10 \times 6 = 60$
Then multiply the **7**	$7 \times 6 = 42$
Finally, add the answers together	**102**

Now try these

7 × 18

6 × 23

8 × 15

9 × 26

Multiplying by 9

If you find multiplying by 9 tricky, an easy way to cope is to multiply by 10 instead and then take one lot away.

> **9 × 15**

$$15 \times 10 = 150$$
$$150 - 15 = 135$$

Multiplying by 11

The same trick works when you multiply by 11. First multiply by 10 but this time add one extra lot.

> **11 × 23**

$$23 \times 10 = 230$$
$$230 + 23 = 253$$

Now try these   **42 × 9**   **27 × 9**   **14 × 11**   **54 × 11**

Multiplying by 25

Multiplying by 25 sounds as if it could be fairly difficult, but it isn't when you remember that four 25s are 100. This means that to multiply by 25 all you have to do is multiply by 100 (add two zeros for whole numbers) and then divide by 4.

> **25 × 16**

Begin by multiplying **16** by **100**	$16 \times 100 = 1600$
Then divide by **4**	$1600 \div 4 = 400$

It won't always be this easy but practice will help.

Carol's tips

66 Here are a few items to remember. Multiples of 2 always end in an even number. With multiples of 3 the sum of the digits will always be divisible by 3. With multiples of 9 the sum of the digits is always divisible by 9. 99

Now try these   **12 × 25**   **24 × 25**   **30 × 25**   **7 × 25**

If you add two odd numbers, the answer is ... guess what? Another even number!

495 = 11 × 45

Answers

Pages 4/5 Addition 1

326 + 218 = 544   457 + 336 = 793   3174 + 1926 = 5100

7 + 8 = 15   6 + 9 = 15   5 + 8 = 13   4 + 3 = 7

6 + 7 = 13   2 + 8 = 10   9 + 5 = 14   7 + 1 = 8

18 + 9 = 27   38 + 7 = 45   24 + 8 = 32   54 + 9 = 63

38 + 19 = 57   65 + 29 = 94   46 + 39 = 85   38 + 59 = 97

Pages 6/7 Addition 2

437 + 265 = 702   743 + 185 = 928   518 + 367 = 885

613 + 192 = 805   304 + 509 = 813   108 + 394 = 502

216 + 494 = 710

27 + 45 = 72   54 + 39 = 93   36 + 57 = 93   63 + 23 = 86

26 + 437 = 463   2453 + 316 = 2769

4.76 + 0.38 = 5.14   3.53 + 1.65 = 5.18

Pages 8/9 Subtraction

43 − 25 = 18   61 − 37 = 24   52 − 16 = 36   86 − 59 = 27

428 − 319 = 109   371 − 154 = 217   517 − 348 = 169

33 − 9 = 24   42 − 11 = 31   42 − 9 = 33

67 − 11 = 56   64 − 9 = 55   33 − 11 = 22

307 − 149 = 158   602 − 435 = 167

470 − 248 = 222   320 − 106 = 214

Pages 10/11 Multiplication 1

146 x 4 = 584   314 x 6 = 1884

265 x 5 = 1325   472 x 7 = 3304

157 x 15 = 2355   123 x 14 = 1722

13 x 20 = 260   14 x 20 = 280   12 x 40 = 480   13 x 50 = 650

18 x 4 = 72   247 x 4 = 988   362 x 4 = 1448   163 x 4 = 652

Pages 12/13 Multiplication 2

3.9 x 7 = 27.3   4.7 x 4 = 18.8

5.5 x 5 = 27.5   8.4 x 8 = 67.2

4.8 x 10 = 48   5.84 x 10 = 58.4   72.3 x 100 = 7230

Pages 14/15 Division 1

$\frac{1}{2}$ of 60 = 30 $\frac{1}{3}$ of 24 = 8 $\frac{1}{4}$ of 80 = 20

$7\overline{)28}$ = 4   56 ÷ 7 = 8   32 ÷ 4 = 8 $6\overline{)36}$ = 6

$8\overline{)594}$ = 74 r 2 $7\overline{)364}$ = 52 $6\overline{)468}$ = 78 $7\overline{)616}$ = 88

Pages 14/15 Division 1 (continued)

$3\overline{)135}$ = 45 $5\overline{)75}$ = 15 $7\overline{)84}$ = 12

$4\overline{)96}$ = 24 $6\overline{)144}$ = 24 $8\overline{)128}$ = 16

Pages 16/17 Division 2

Minibus question: Answer 2.

Vase question: Answer 6.

47 ÷ 10 = 4.7   1245 ÷ 100 = 12.45   1711 ÷ 1000 = 1.711

$18\overline{)417}$ = 23 r 3 or 23 $\frac{3}{18}$ or 23 $\frac{1}{6}$

$23\overline{)481}$ = 20 r 21 or 20 $\frac{21}{23}$ $36\overline{)845}$ = 23 r 17 or 23 $\frac{17}{36}$

Pages 18/19 Times tables

6 x 7 = 42   4 x 9 = 36   8 x 5 = 40   6 x 8 = 48

6 x 13 = 78   9 x 14 = 126   7 x 15 = 105   4 x 19 = 76

Pages 20/21 Special numbers

3 x 9 = 27   7 x 9 = 63   8 x 9 = 72   9 x 9 = 81

1, 2, 4, 8, **16**   1, 2, 4, 5, 10, **20**

1, 2, 4, 7, 14, **28**   1, 2, 4, 8, 16, **32**

Pages 22/23 Fun challenges

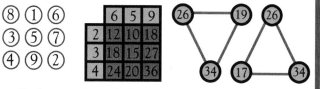

Find two numbers which total 9 and give a product of 20.
Answer 4 and 5.

Which two numbers have a product of 21 and a difference of 4?
Answer 3 and 7.

Two numbers have a total of 35 but have a difference of 7. What
are the two numbers? Answer 14 and 21.

The product of two numbers is 63 and the difference between
them is 2. What are the numbers? Answer 7 and 9.

In your head! Answer 8.

= 14 squares

14 21 28 35 **42 49**   17 9 1 **-7 -15 -23**

4000 2000 1000 **500 250**   1 2 4 7 11 **16 22 29**

3 5 9 17 33 **65 129 257**   1 1 2 3 5 8 **13 21 34**

1 2 5 10 20 **50 1 2** English coins

31 28 31 30 **31 30 31 31** Number of days in the
months of the year.

Pages 24/25 Algebra & Brackets

$10 \times 6 = 60$ $24 - 9 = 15$ $32 \div 4 = 8$

1. Jamie's number is 14   2. $x = 9$ 3. $x = 4$

$7x = 63$ $x = 9$ $19 + x = 50$ $x = 31$

$x - 12 = 8$ $x = 20$

$6 + (4 \times 3) = 18$ $(6 + 4) \times 3 = 30$

$12 \div (4 + 2) = 2$ $(12 \div 4) + 2 = 5$

Pages 26/27 Perimeter & Area

Perimeter of a room that measures 2.5 m by 3.2 m = 11.4 m.

Perimeter of a garden that is 15 m by 12 m = 54 m.

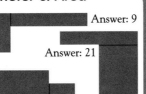

Answer: 9

Answer: 21

What is the area of a field that is 40 m by 60 m? = 2400 m².

What is the area of a book cover that is 11 cm by 15 cm? = 165 cm²   Answer: 16

Pages 28/29 Ratio & Proportion

One for every 10 = 1 : 10   Two for every 15 = 2 : 15

One for every 20 = 1 : 20   Three for every 11 = 3 : 11

What is the ratio of green to blue in each shape?

5 : 3   4 : 2 or 2 : 1   2 : 7   3 : 2   1 : 3

$4 : 5 = \frac{4}{5}$ $3 : 10 = \frac{3}{10}$ $4 : 7 = \frac{4}{7}$ $8 : 12 = \frac{8}{12}$ or $\frac{2}{3}$

5 in every 8 = 5 : 8 swimmers are girls.

3 in every 8 = 3 : 8 swimmers with yellow costumes.

2 in every 8 = 2 : 8 swimmers with blue caps.

1. 30 children in the class.

2. The ratio of milk to plain is 3 : 2.

Pages 30/31 Fractions

$\frac{1}{3}$ of 24 = 8 $\frac{1}{5}$ of 30 = 6

$\frac{1}{10}$ of 90 = 9 $\frac{1}{4}$ of 28 = 7

$\frac{4}{8} = \frac{1}{2}$ $\frac{6}{15} = \frac{2}{5}$ $\frac{5}{20} = \frac{1}{4}$ $\frac{10}{50} = \frac{1}{5}$

$\frac{5}{7}$ of 21 = 15 $\frac{4}{9}$ of 36 = 16 $\frac{3}{4}$ of 24 = 18 $\frac{4}{5}$ of 30 = 24

$\frac{14}{3} = 4\frac{2}{3}$ $\frac{12}{5} = 2\frac{2}{5}$ $\frac{16}{6} = 2\frac{4}{6}$ or $2\frac{2}{3}$

$\frac{13}{2} = 6\frac{1}{2}$ $\frac{7}{2} = 3\frac{1}{2}$ $\frac{11}{4} = 2\frac{3}{4}$ $\frac{19}{3} = 6\frac{1}{3}$

Pages 32/33 Decimals

155.6 cm = 156 cm   7.1 kg = 7 kg   99.5 grams = 100 grams

$0.72 = \frac{18}{25}$ $0.45 = \frac{9}{20}$ $0.64 = \frac{16}{25}$ $0.8 = \frac{20}{25}$ $0.35 = \frac{7}{20}$

$\frac{1}{5} = 0.2$ $\frac{2}{5} = 0.4$ $\frac{1}{4} = 0.25$ $\frac{3}{4} = 0.75$ $\frac{4}{5} = 0.8$

$\frac{3}{10} = 0.3$ $\frac{7}{10} = 0.7$ $\frac{4}{8} = 0.5$ $\frac{3}{5} = 0.6$

Pages 34/35 Percentages

43% of £1.00 = 43p   93% of 1 metre = 93 cm

37% of £1.00 = 37p   84% of 1 metre = 84 cm

With the extra 20% the bottle will hold 720 ml.

What percentage of 60 is 12? Answer 20%.

What percentage of 30 is 15? Answer 50%.

What percentage of 10 is 9? Answer 90%.

Pages 36/37 Squares & Cubes

$15^2 = 225$ $13^2 = 169$ $12^2 = 144$ $7^2 = 49$

12 m × 12 m = 144 m   10 cm × 10 cm = 100 cm

15 m × 15 m = 225 m   6 cm × 6 cm = 36 cm

$10^3 = 1000$ $8^3 = 512$ $1^3 = 1$

$15^3 = 3375$ $7^3 = 343$ $11^3 = 1331$

Pages 38/39 Negative numbers

$4 - 9 = -5$ $-1 - 4 = -5$ $1 - 4 = -3$

$3 - 7 = -4$ $2 - 8 = -6$ $-5 - 5 = -10$

What Celsius temperature is shown on each thermometer?

18°C drops to 16°C   15°C drops to 13°C

−10°C drops to −12°C   −2°C drops to −4°C

UNITED KINGDOM 5°C   SPAIN 9°C   FRANCE 2°C   GERMANY −2°C

$6 - 7 = -1$ $8 - 2 = 6$ $-3 - 1 = -4$

$-2 + 2 = 0$ $-2 + 4 = 2$ $-5 + 6 = 1$

$-1 + 6 = 5$ $-9 + 2 = -7$ $-7 + 4 = -3$

Pages 40/41 Co-ordinates

Square 4 spaces to the right:
(0, 4); (0, 1); (3, 4); (3, 1)

Sloping shape 2 spaces to the left:
(0, 1); (3, 1); (−2, −2); (1, −2)

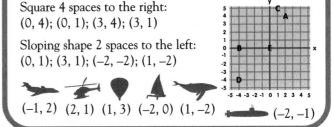

(−1, 2)   (2, 1)   (1, 3)   (−2, 0)   (1, −2)   (−2, −1)

Pages 42/43 Checking answers

£5.08 × 14 = £71.12   286 × 9 = 2574

712 ml × 19 = 13528 ml

The correct answer is:

$\begin{array}{r} 726 \\ -447 \\ \hline 279 \end{array}$

156 × 26 = 4056   263 × 47 = 12361

648 × 59 = 38232   174 × 75 = 13050

Pages 44/45 Carol's maths tricks

Doubles 32   128   50   104   74   146   98   162

Halves 21   12   39   42   18   46

7 × 18 = 126   6 × 23 = 138   8 × 15 = 120

9 × 26 = 234   42 × 9 = 378   27 × 9 = 243

14 × 11 = 154   54 × 11 = 594   12 × 25 = 300

24 × 25 = 600   30 × 25 = 750   7 × 25 = 175

Index

Numbers in **bold** refer to topic pages.

Acknowledgments

Dorling Kindersley would like to thank the following people for their help in the production of this book: Sheila Hanly, John Kennedy, Penny York, Caroline Greene, Howie Cruthes, Martin Wilson, Ben Morgan, and Lester Cheeseman.

Picture credits
The publisher would like to thank the following for their kind permission to reproduce their photograph:
Barrie Watts: 44 top right.

Sean McArdle is Head Teacher at a primary school. He has degrees in Education and Primary Assessment and has taught maths for many years. Sean has also written maths test books, workbooks, practice papers, and course books.

Carol Vorderman, who first made her name performing lightning calculations on television, has a Masters Degree in Engineering from Cambridge University. She is totally committed to popularizing and communicating maths and science, and writes on these subjects for national newspapers. Carol appears regularly on maths and science television programmes on Channel 4, ITV, and the BBC.

X	1	2	3	4	5	6	7	8	9	10	11	12
1	1	2	3	4	5	6	7	8	9	10	11	12
2	2	4	6	8	10	12	14	16	18	20	22	24
3	3	6	9	12	15	18	21	24	27	30	33	36
4	4	8	12	16	20	24	28	32	36	40	44	48
5	5	10	15	20	25	30	35	40	45	50	55	60
6	6	12	18	24	30	36	42	48	54	60	66	72
7	7	14	21	28	35	42	49	56	63	70	77	84
8	8	16	24	32	40	48	56	64	72	80	88	96
9	9	18	27	36	45	54	63	72	81	90	99	108
10	10	20	30	40	50	60	70	80	90	100	110	120
11	11	22	33	44	55	66	77	88	99	110	121	132
12	12	24	36	48	60	72	84	96	108	120	132	144